HORNMAN

URBAN LIFE CENTER
5240 SOUTH   AVENUE

CHICAGO, IL 60615

Property Of
Chicago Center
1515 E. 52nd Pl, Chicago, IL
773-363-1012
www.chicagocenter.org

HORNMAN

STERLING PLUMPP

Sterling D. Plumpp
Best Wishes
2-13-97

Horn Man

Copyright © 1995 Sterling Plumpp

All rights reserved. No part of this book may be reproduced, stored in retrieval systems or transmitted in any form, by any means, including mechanical, electronic, photocopying, recording, or otherwise without prior written permission of the publisher.

Published by Third World Press, P.O. Box 19730, Chicago, IL 60619

Library of Congress Catalog Card Number: 94-61822
ISBN: 0-88378-177-8

Cover Art and Design by Craig A. Taylor
Manufactured in the United States
94 95 96 97 98 99   8 7 6 5 4 3 2 1

For Von Freeman, Boptized

Table of Contents

Part I
NAME GAME

1. Be-Bop
2. Soul Finder
3. Every Day
4. Boptism

Part II
SANCTUARY

Part III
SOLOS

Part IV
END ZONE

1. Thirty-two Buckets of Bop
2. Too Much To Read

Von Freeman

Part I
NAME GAME

Be-Bop

1.
    Be-Bop is precise clumsiness.
      Awkward lyricism
        under a feather's control.
A world in a crack.
Seen by ears.
      Von Freeman's
tenor Apocalypses/beginning
skies fussy about air and protective
    of trombones on Jacob's Ladder
      strung from basses
in a corner of handclaps.
Drums praying over evil
    done by trumpets
    and dances in fingertips.
Be-Bop is elusive hammerlocks
a piano accords crescendos
    in blue moanings.
Lingers in beats marching
    across faces of sense.
Harmonic nightmares obeying
    pianissimos of tones
erupting from barks of Powell.
Be-Bop is unexpected
    style punching music
with garlic in tempo.

        Billie's pain

and a cup of insinuations
drunk by laughter
before tears arise.

Soul Finder

2.
Drama. Late
tides of history
in Von Freeman
on a tenor voyage
to cells of yester
day. A mood
harbinger. The
Mississippi and
Nile dancing as
long shadows of
his Mojo hands.
Reach
for Bird's discus
of synthesis reigning
over heavens
of barbed wire/Prez
stretched be
low his crescendos of
innovation. With
the blues in
toning ancestry. Misty
appears on wheels
of a chariot/the
drummer is urging.
For Satchmo/with
his left hand/for
Bags/with his right.

He
takes off his mask of thunder
and lyrics
coliseums and monuments
with wind. Then
reeds the Promised
Land from a dark
cavern of quivering
flesh his fingers
pinch with genius.
World of the spirit,
horn man/playing
the beginning all
hushed in his hand.
Land of the spirit,
horn man; he plays
a time/the gods under
stand.

Every Day

3.
Every day.
Every day.

A tenor ax crosses
over my mind.

The cantankerous
nomenclature he holds
over rebellions in voice.

(Ordered.

Hyphenated scars
he deciphers
on lonely roads of solos.

Speaking in
bric
brac
tongues of desire.
Some
thing a snake hisses
at his elbow.

Now
he sees over a smoke filled
sound. At a place by a corner
in dreams.

He
some
times breathes a ballad of
silence.

A parqueted window
opens against the fire
he swallows.

An epic
of intervals inside his moods.
A
be-bopper flung on a low sky.

An a cappella scavenger
of goodtimes. He can count

sun
downs
in his father's name.
If
silence does not foreclose
on time.

A stevedore whistles
his burdens to steps
of an unseen drummer
in night's hands.

As he
    cuts ribbonic melody

between claps his memory
beats on tones

    salt peanuts
can scream inside a yard bird.

Vilifying

    standards

with lyrics from births
inside and inside and inside
his ax's vision

Boptism

4.
I know where I am going.
Open
gates winding memory.
A ballad is a fortress
I introduce. Bird's lineage.
A barb-wire guardrail a
round a bridge
where I confess explosive messages.

Meaning.

I go alone.

Though a drummer
accompanies with soft distances
in his electrocuted rhythms.

An exodus

from when
I go back
to where I began.

A trombone folds
envelopes of wind and
dresses in brass cloaks.
An artistry of turmoil, belonging
to closed eyes.

The bridge
is my minister. Open arms
under tides. Miles
d
o
w
n
tracks of depths. My second
home is across something.
Towards
fractured seconds
I hit with the wind.

Memory is a terror. Shadow
with madness. Post
bop celebrant I am. Miles
from Houdini twisting lyrics
from open palms of bullets.
Santa Claus brings me
each year.

      Post bop
celebrant with night
over my eyes. Behind
excursions where I scouted
for a future. A tradition of
bones I suck dry. A totem of
treasons I feel when I speak.

All my people's dreams.
All my people's hopes.
All my people's joys.

I dance. Leaning

from a piano which begs

for a license to cross.
Remember who is my minister?
I gotta ask him for a revival.
I collect his permits.

Deep river.
Deep river.

I got miles over yonder
past a half century
the Brooklyn Bridge chained
my name.

Meaning.

I go alone.

Through calypso passages.
Through sharpness of identity.
Through ropes and whips.
To blues with a purpose.

I just come from the barrel.
I just come from the barrel.

Wailing

a slab of tokens
for my debts.

Bird, you messenger.
Bird, you path-finder.
Bird, you ghetto Moses.
Bird, you road-mapper.

Trane, you prophetic loner.
Trane, you inventor.
Trane, you horticulturist of tones.
Trane, you ritualist master.

You bop-tized me
with a tenor ax.

At the place where a guitar
assists legends in my childhood.
Searching for songs at the lost
and found.

And I limbo over the graffiti
of air to a slaughterhouse
where I trade murders for the screams
my horn breathes on night

Part II
Sanctuary

1.
The meeting in sections.

Acres of laughter. Miles
around tenor migrations.

An explorer,

        who traverses

minutes in sounds. Officiates.

He is a cartographer of wind
crisscrossing prairies of self.
A birdwatching renegade
pleating lines from myths.

Dry bones murmur whirlwinds from in
side horns. A place of
the soul vented by insights.
Where The Monk inside tenements of pauses

interprets rituals he wears round
edges of his shadow.

2.
Bird is the word.
Coltrane is the thing.
Is his ceremonial gift.
A wisecracking riff
side thunder's head.
A ballad opening
inside its core
for troubled wanderers.
Some low blues with razor
in hand to chase pain away.
Horns queued like young bodies
at mortuaries. To force reflection.
To define mirrors for history's face.

3.
The Apartment is a sanctuary
where music rises from crowded silences
to stand by hearts.

4.
A trumpet's hasty recitations
or a trombone's leisured speech
or a French horn's elongated brass utterances.

All. Forewarned to brevity.

Bird is the word.
Coltrane is the thing.

Not length.

5.
Axmen file past after stretching breath
and fingers. For larger dreams
in spaces of longings.
Each an interpreter.
Each a handyman

        for the globe.

The Explorer holds at the end of his solo's
voyage across night's expansive boundaries.

6.
Rover man.
Rover man.

You got anchors in your hands
like a plowman. Empty spaces
are your fields. The air is rich
soil behind your closed eyes of rows.
Where you cover memories
in them. Then reach
across my grandfather's denials
to sprinkle hopes over crushed dreams.
You do
that with your left hand.

A revivalist of distances, you mediate
worlds from a basement near a corner
in the mythology of your gestures.
Memory sits there with a glass
half full of dreams; half empty
of loneliness. I carve for my lines.
Mourner's benches are absent.
Adjacent to barstools. You, a deacon of
wild streets where violence is bartered
for by palms of self-hatred, summon melody.
You are a revivalist
who gathers thread from air
to stitch meanings from bits of
sarcasm and genius. So your congregation
is bound, drawn closer, locked in embraces
with the breeze you call onto them.

Rover man.
Rover man.

You comfort journeys others marry.
There are paths in your face, maps,
overlays of the imagination.

7.
All about laughter over pain.
(A half telephone for sale.

A quartet. This singular tenor's rampages.
Chicago pathfinder strutting on broken glass
and bricks. So much live talk and the advice
of curtains. Pulled over opportunities.
Each a night/a leap year from evolutions
in his speech. Jug's big hits
among my foolishness where tomorrows
climb on bones of nightscarred lynchings.
Ascend heavens where my songs elicit
their metaphors from blood. And, clocks
I teach, affirm time I conjure. Night
after night, landscapes offer pilgrims
a place to dream. (all my wife-in-laws
on parade.

The tall anticipation of oak
spreads over: you can help yourself,
baby, you can rise...

8.
A sermon behind distances.
Saliva
and hallelujahs.
Creek long as
the river in his eyes.

Muddy legends
near surface.

Generations of down
trodden solos rise
in his memory. Night
in
gales sing recalcitrance
over his face.

Broke confessions
reign
in kingdoms of his movements.

9.
Speaking
in vamps over dark beverages
his father drank from tomorrows.
Speaking
in tongues his mother
threaded crises to patch
her montage of troubles.

Here I go.
Here I go.
Here I go.

Tenderloin
stretched over fingers. A la carte
strings, nephews
of a guitar's reputation
in nuances Charlie Christian
liberated under fall leaves
of another crossroads.

10.
Here a whole sky
cries inside my bones,
his trumpet, revolting tons
he tries to scream
but can not. His song muted;
hubcaps talk in fragments
of his spirit.

I struggle
to keep my father out
side the lyric I witness
in the horrors. Time permits
him to blow.

Going without tracks.
Going without tracks.
Going without tracks.

11.
His guitar
puts a basket under ears
to catch day
break. A basement poem
treading eyelids of a long
winter tunnel. A bad shadow,
headless/crying over invisible
dry bones.

A picture.
A score.
An open door.

Organ and guitar
drafting petitions
to foreclose on legacy.
Under a drummer's hearings.

Long
ways from the crusade
of park benches
where the crows kept company
in separate foot
notes of estrangement.

12.
There is still morality here. Fingers across
apocalypses/recall faces
of queens in brown incognito.
At the school of pain
he grants diplomas

with pulverized phrases
he spittons on air.

Open-mouthed.

He unhands a guitar's lease
on the stairs of loneliness.

Offers commentary
with the wit of sweat.

13.
Jimmy I remember
on kool-aid and pluck* days
in GI incarceration. My imagination

out there in some place
where VF's history
spills outside the universe
of cocoons he sleeps winters.

I
come horn every ten years
or
so

in a night's voyages

---

*Pluck is white port wine we used to buy in great abundance at the end of the month while I was in the Army. We colored it with kool-aid as a delicacy.

Von Freeman

Part III
SOLOS

1.
Captain gave me time. Captain
gave me a place. I survey marrow
each night I blow. Each sound
is a microscope. Seeing eyes
for days ahead. I am a commandant of
caravans. The road is my navel
issued by pellets of blood. I
follow.

My saxophone is a key.
A collaged territory of
witnesses. To appear
before triumphs of bad luck.

For if you are a shadow
the approach of night is a day
break. Your existence crouched in limbos
stretching into scenes. A sax
man lectures on in his moods.

The tenor is God's voices:
  Let
  there be Dinahs with my days
  plaited in her troubles.
  Let there be Bessies on banks
  singing steps from hours.
  Let
  there be Satchmos with deep rivers
  flowing from his smile. A delta of moaners
  rising around ankles of the old men's dances.

For
when the moon steps out in over
alls I get happy.

2.
He plays bingo with skulls.
Alone. In a crowded room. To
night.
A crane swings out digits
with hammerings. Where pilings of
tones are liberated zones of dreams.
Peace. A whole lotta self
unbound from distance pain
measures in epochs of stones.
Rubbed against my name. Style
as saboteurs. A willingness
to remember codes dry bones calcified
in holidays. Where my spirit raises
pennants over tentacles of jails.
Where midnight birds are clad
in charcoal vespers. And the honey
suckle is an exile in their ghosts of
pulverized sentences. For trivial light in
side their anchors of will.

Ninety-nine miles from nowhere.

3.
The horn is a body, a part of every
body. History recoiled in night
mares where pilgrims are locked up.
It, a sleeve of cauldron marches,
breathes tonics, irrigated salves
the root man and herb woman left off.
By riffs brass and winds
have come to know in after hours of
The Memory. Where this arm rushes
from iron and ashes with wishes.
It speaks and creation occurs:
old settlements kidnapped by floods
rise in tides on Bessie Smith's chest.
Moaning
in tempo of clapped hands round
midnites of prayers. He blows.
As he fills souls with lyrics
he accompanies to their wounds.
Takes
off his scarf and soaks discord
from flesh.
Pats
his right foot
while bowed in his medical pose.
It
vaccinates, his horn.

Shouts

4.
Each night.
I play. I go somewhere
else, come here and gone to yonder times.
Bringing ways to see
with my tones. I was born
in nineteen switchblade night.

You,
      there outside memory,
come in

to aisles where touches read
the loneliness inside.

My sax

exploits its open policy of
enrollment.

                            Tutor claims
broken hearts must pass.

You,

    there off in
to bottom of your glass.

Come in

to these mirrors I blow
from hunting grounds in travels.
I am a wanderer.

I am from this little place
called Whichaway Long Road
where I get letters from light monthly

and had to telegram the sun

5.
Piece of downcast cries
out there. Eyes with deserts
where tears laughed. I know you.
No name raindrops out there.
Crying sand into hours. I know
you, honey. I know you and I
know your laughter too. God
bless the child that got
his trials. Miss Heart Broken
Loneliness out there. God bless and
Bless. Bless bless bless orders
from inside crying dry insides. Bless.
I know. The heart marvels. The green out
lets even deserts can't swallow. I believe.
I believe and I know there are doors in you.
There is something inside; some
thing you can ride from the cave hurts impose.
That's why I play. I drag bottom of the floor.
To pick you up and hand you this rose. That's why
I blow. I drag the floor. And I know. And I
believe there is something inside. My music can
give a ride from bruises and pains you try to
hide. I believe and I know, Babe, I just blow
and blow and blow.

6.
All paths lead to pain
but you gotta dance them.
I cry.
I ache.
I hurt.
But I never flop down.
Cause joy always in the corridor out
side gloom. You, Mister
Ragtime wrapped head
over there. I can stop
you from crying on the stool.
I
can rub out spots on your dreams
so you can ease out clothes of sorrows
where the Miss Boss Man in your life
chopped wood on your expectations.
I got your penitentiary of dirges
right here. I can cut its hair
with longings I carry in ballads.

Those dragons of put
downs on your neck I can chew on
in my solo's voyages to out
skirts of death. Cause I never for
get that laughter escorts tears
if you play the music so they can dance.
Where everybody swims like good
time hymns where yesterdays' storm
is quieted by rhythms of prayers.
One half block from the slave ship
I practice riffs on and sleep
with pain each night I lie down

but wake up with my sword
at bad luck's throat

7.
Loneliness shacks up
with my appetite. Here
where death is a close neighbour.
And the watch I hide
in sweaty palms
keeps vigil over crying
as a form of happiness. If
you can blow it. Here
I use my ax as a jump
rope: last night and the night
before. Twenty-four birds
at my door. I git up
let them in. That's how
Be-Bop begins. This journey
I take between flesh sweats
cribs for bumps and grinds
to nap on. Where the wilderness
behind my closed eyes I translate
into a chordal geography of landscape
I follow. This horn I blow.
This sax I am. This sax
I am. This sax I am

8.
I sit here in a caboose and
reed directions to engines of time.
Whining toward somewhere
beyond my ear. I got this Magna
Cum lowdown feeling where judge
accused me of migraine laziness
and awarded my name Phi Beta
Kappa disgrace. Where men sit
drinking 99 proof and talking
to 199 proof in skirts beside
them. I bring music which is
a transfer after yours done
expired on a cold night. I
cover waterfronts on my baby's
face and seek Bud with callings
just off the Pea Vine Special.
Where Elmo dusted his broom side.
I sit here. A collator of fallen
burdens inside my sax. Making timber,
Lord, making timber

9.
A pick
pocket of other folks' troubles.
Roaming
in terrible lyrics.

                        Summertime
and the funerals are high.

Always.
On.
On the porch of dreams.
Beyond the telescope's eye.
Always.
I
saw him arrest a quartet of minstrels
on their knees in a cartoon. With
warrants from choir buoys

he directs in his moans. Looking in
side
him
self
always.

                        Looking a
head with your pain tutored
by findings of chords.

In The Prohibited Land of Senses.

Where he domesticates herds of demons
with stencils from his fingers. There is
a grammar of lore on his face
where whispers of clouds in labor
reside.

Summertime and the funerals are high.
Summertime and the funerals are high.

Hell on my party line and telephones down
in heaven.

10.
I was buried in a peanut shell
where Caldonia pawns corners
with Zora's hands on her hips.
I
resurrect in fourteen howls
with Muddy Waters trading shots
with Old Scappy at Pap Silas's
cemetery. I was found guilty of
improvisation by Just Going On.
The Prosecutor. Out on a fifty
cigarette bail The Handy Man
argued for on The Night Train.
Puffing down the line. In some
old woman's prayers. Her baby gone
from the Big Boss Man's debts.
The hot sun and a cross
cut saw appeal liberty of my bones
and I leap on a high balling strike
by Satchel. Slide to home
plate at Theresa's on 47th and
the basement of hobos. Rise

to feed my ax my terrors
for a song

11.
I
always make my wings too
soon. Because of unconscious
distances I come
from.

Throbbing
in crowded shadows.
Looking
for a place for stillness.

A wanderer. My father
says.

I did not own
any land but my father
and my mother
were language owners
and their fathers and mothers
were language owners.

They took me
on wagon rides in their pain;
I sit in the back
blowing tonic of their might
into my chilled hands.

The drumbeat of names
they whispered. Still claps.
When I hit a beat.
You hear God
knocking on your heart.

They ask.

Time it
self dances.

Opening choruses.

Where I commit my mornings
to downtrodden alibis.

Still laughter.

Remember.

Time it
self dances.

When dreams smash stones
and even steel cries.
A
l
o
n
e
I, wander

12.
Out on a solitary limb of wind
where I ante up my spirit
for draw poker with death. The silence
with a straight for eternity. If I
come up ballads I win. Pack
up my little corners of loneliness
I find. Riff long massacres from eyes
crying riverways for the boat I ride.
Till I fling my cells to air
with Bird against a Prezed by
line stars form nodding their light.
And Miles backs in pulling
his moods of spilled ink
over heaven. Counting his steps
to seven. Then descending and
backing up again. Into an
other sky extended subdued under
statements I tenorly paint
on his mask. Each night I
gather my chips of soul

swear to wager solos
at some gate of stares

13.
Over bones of distance
Over sometimes I feel like nobody
Over hip-hop Bibles
Over backseats in history
Over piece a paper in my hand
Over years on Parchman Farm
Over Robben Island
Over Jim Crow
Over Apartheid
Over the dues I owe
Over overcoming
Over vultures in disguise
Over poems in aches
Over piles of lore
Over 'Fessor of hard knocks
Over diplomas
Over admissions
Over depths inside palms

Over handclaps
Over buddies on the run
Over polls of treachery
Over bullet teachings
Over highwayed sermons
Over nineteen years old
Over juke
Over recognition
Over going down slow
Over tin pan alley
Over agony inside shuffling feet
Over my legacy
Over yo bro
Over howdy howdy
Over testifying hands
Over Lucille's open door crying
Over BB's finger-rinsed tales
Over mercy on its knees
Over yo bro
Over silent generations
Over sayings on ironing boards
Over directions in run down shoes

Over Alabama mushrooms
Over yo bro
Over nigger nigger
Over ropes
Over nigger nigger
Over hit the sucker again
Over closed eyes
Over thefts from death
Over vampiric images
Over nigger nigger
Over secrets kept
Over snake eyes
Over skulls
Over awakenings
Over ghosts
Over holy run down shacks
Over inventions

Over blues ponds ignored
Over graffiti on souls
Over silhouettes of hurt
Over skeletons of worry
Over nigger nigger
Over unplowed wastelands in spirits
Over lilacs
Over tears for fruits
Over black rain falling
Over overcoming yesterday
Over crossroads
Over maps of genocide in wrinkles
Over nappy years
Over suns
Over drums

Over a geography of pain
Over solos
Over choruses
Over mountain peaks
Over Amandlas
Over names I named
Over chromatic callings
Over harmonicas
Over shebeen lyrics
Over unknown wanderers
Over singers
Over insanity
Over long longings
Over distances
Over fences
Over tall winds
Over Mississippi mud
Over strange fruits
Over muddied wonder

Over questioning scars
Over who done gone
Over where shall I go
Over what the dream said to daybreak
Over why haints come stepping in
Over when I get to the city
Over whichaways of blood callings
Over dimensions
Over pain covered up
Over mosaics of women in struggle
Over Harriet
Over Winnie Nomzamo
Over Nzinga
Over tenants reaping dust
Over laborers with nowhere to sleep
Over women alone
Over pallets of mercy
Over sweat
Over nuances
Over pulpits
Over eagles flying on Friday
Over drowning on dry land
Over a master plan

Over tapping to Rap
Over yo bro
Over genius abbreviated
Over excellence
Over ashes
Over improvisations
Over the goodfoot
Over got something for you baby
Over big boss man
Over bad bad whiskey
Over cotton sacks
Over flooded hopes
Over sunnyland
Over tell me how long the train been gone

Over fat mamas
Over passionate throbs
Over fat mamas
Over sweet sweet touches
Over flags
Over defiance
Over clenched fists
Over picture shows
Over for colored signs
Over Sowetos
Over children
Over futures
Over firing squads
Over nigger nigger
Over the watusi
Over languages
Over mashed potatoes
Over weeping at holes in the ground
Over hooded assassins

Over outside places
Over lynchings
Over names stolen
Over cayenne pepper in eyes
Over lynchings
Over moral vagrancy
Over the wind accusing
Over hollering insides
Over goober dust
Over trials
Over Nat Turner's vision
Over alphabetic cries
Over volcanic repercussions
Over nicknames
Over heads pushed down
Over crutches of time
Over I wanna be your personal manager baby
Over panther changed gangs
Over my names
Over yeahs
Over amens

Over say it loud
Over Lordy Lordys
Over Lord have mercys
Over triangles of moans
Over a place without a place
Over my soul
Over fast talking space
Over daddy-yos
Over echoes from tightening ropes
Over nigger nigger
Over yo bro
Over saxophone heaven
Over tenor gatekeeper
Over alto usher

Over yo bro
Over saxophone heaven
Over alto usher
Over tenor gatekeeper

There are no exits in memory

Part IV
END ZONE

Thirty-two Buckets of Bop

1.
This is the quest beyond silences
where mountains are inventions.
Where islands reside
in dreams and dreams.

The hereafter.
As affirmation. The blues

hung over chasms.
Debts
excavate. A calendar of hurts.
Ellison subpoenas
for his invisible parlor of the nameless.

Two
steps behind the veil
DuBois coils in psalms
with licorice nightsticks of moans

to beat mornings from lullabyes
chains swore to darkness.

A hornman barters
with St. Peter. At the gaze of trumpets.
Miles, wide legged,
shoulders arched for myths,

interprets the numbers:

thirty-two buckets of bop
for a pinch of salt and one soul.

To board the Trane somewhere
above heaven in low keys
and chordal disturbances. Sit-ins
by Max. Mister PC on freedom
rides in lowlands of sorrow.

This minister of laughter
and satire. Re-invents legends.
The saxophone as womb. Tenor as mother.
His sounds are wife-in-laws.
Sitting, notebooks in hands,

to capture tales they inside
tumbling in distances he blows
for a ballad's intoxicated bit of sense.

He blows.
He blows.

The nights into volumes

Too Much To Read

2.
In some forlorn magazine in
side his eyes. Diagonal paths
in pain.

      This
mauve

architect wandering behind nightshades
structures lineages. I prayed for.

A poet of seams and mortar. Crying in

side rafters I cling to between centuries.

A griot of travels inside self.
          Admits
to forty-four years of rites.
Horns testifying.
Legacy of Bird.
Magic into selves.

Magic.

Short bursts of sorrow
for the joy, sermons
emit over silenced glasses.

Von.
A
Free
man quilts longings into blankets. Roads for an other day.

Here I am.
Here I am.
Here I am.

Lexicons of his fingers shout
before a congregation of head
nods.

Too much.
Too much and
too much

to read